Contents

Welcome! 3

Unit 1: My Garden 7

Unit 2: My School.................. 12

Unit 3: At the Farm 17

Unit 4: At Home 22

Unit 5: My Day 27

Unit 6: At the Beach 32

Unit 7: A Day Out.................. 37

Unit 8: Animals 42

Vocabulary Review 47

Welcome!

Welcome Unit, Lesson 1: Song

3

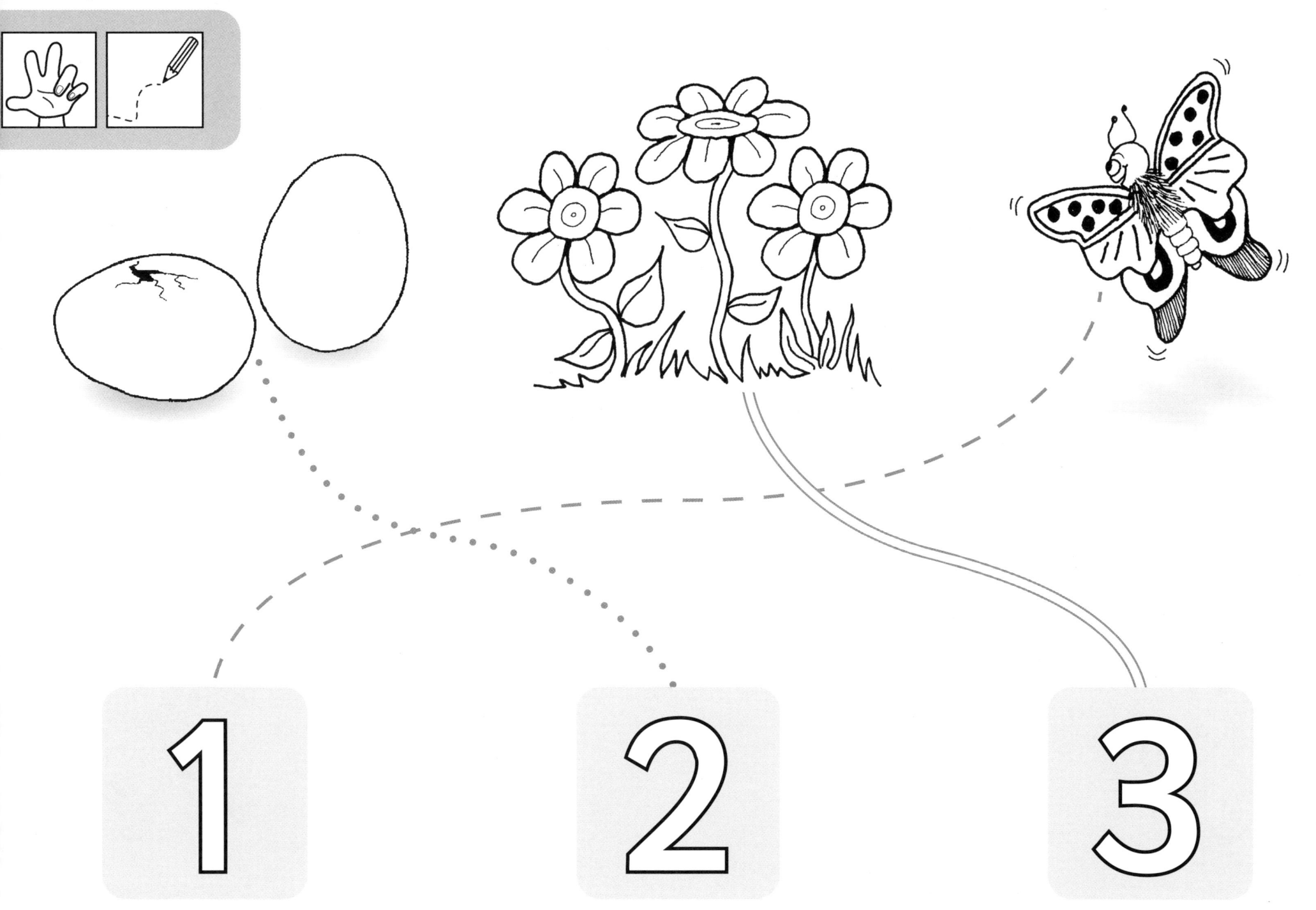

Welcome Unit, Lesson 3: Chant

My Garden

Unit 1, Lesson 1: Vocabulary

Unit 1, Lesson 2: Vocabulary

Unit 1, Lesson 3: Story

Review 1: /s/, /a/, /t/

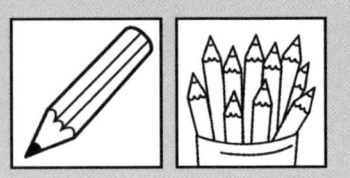

My School

1. 2. 3.

Unit 2, Lesson 1: Vocabulary

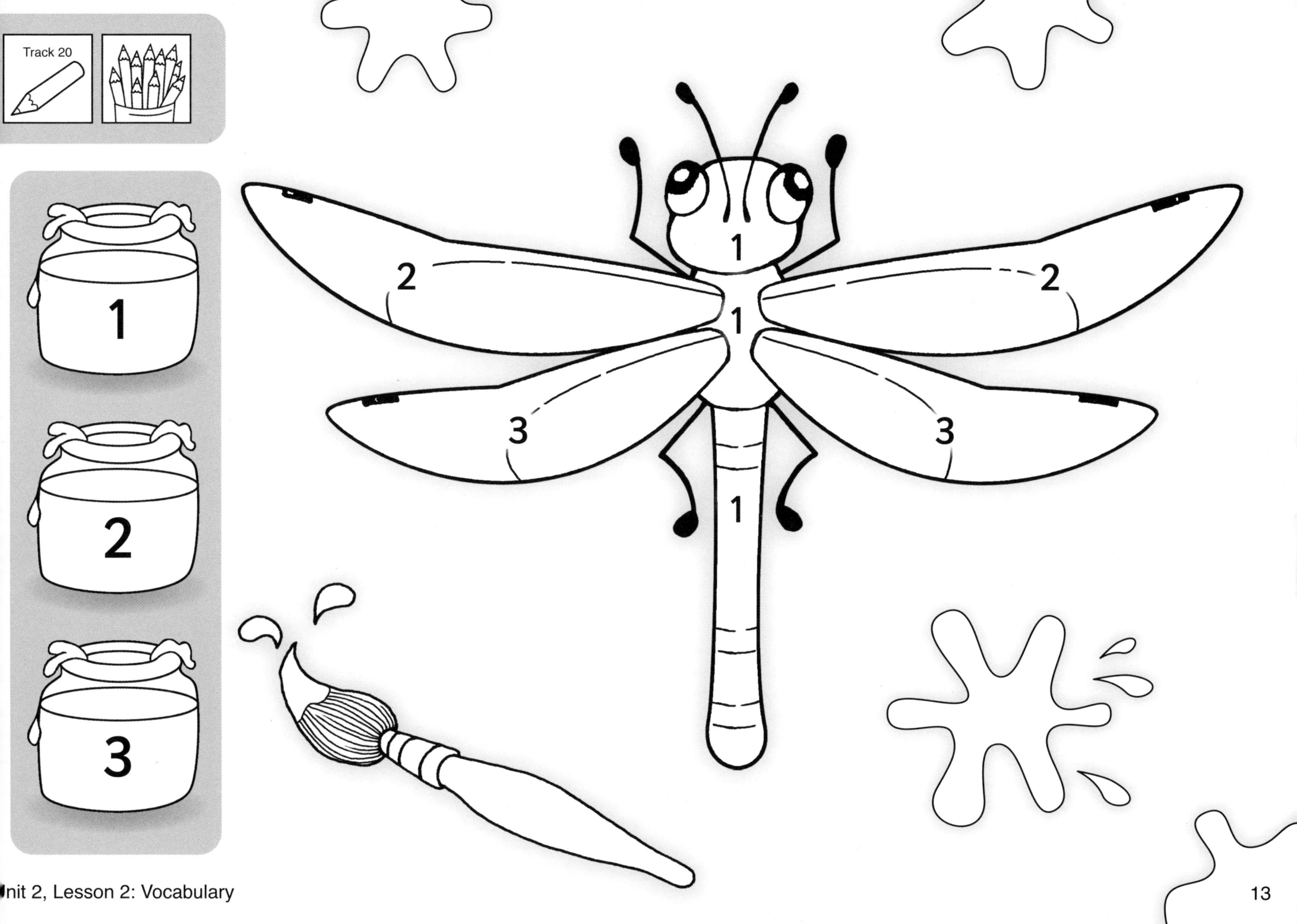

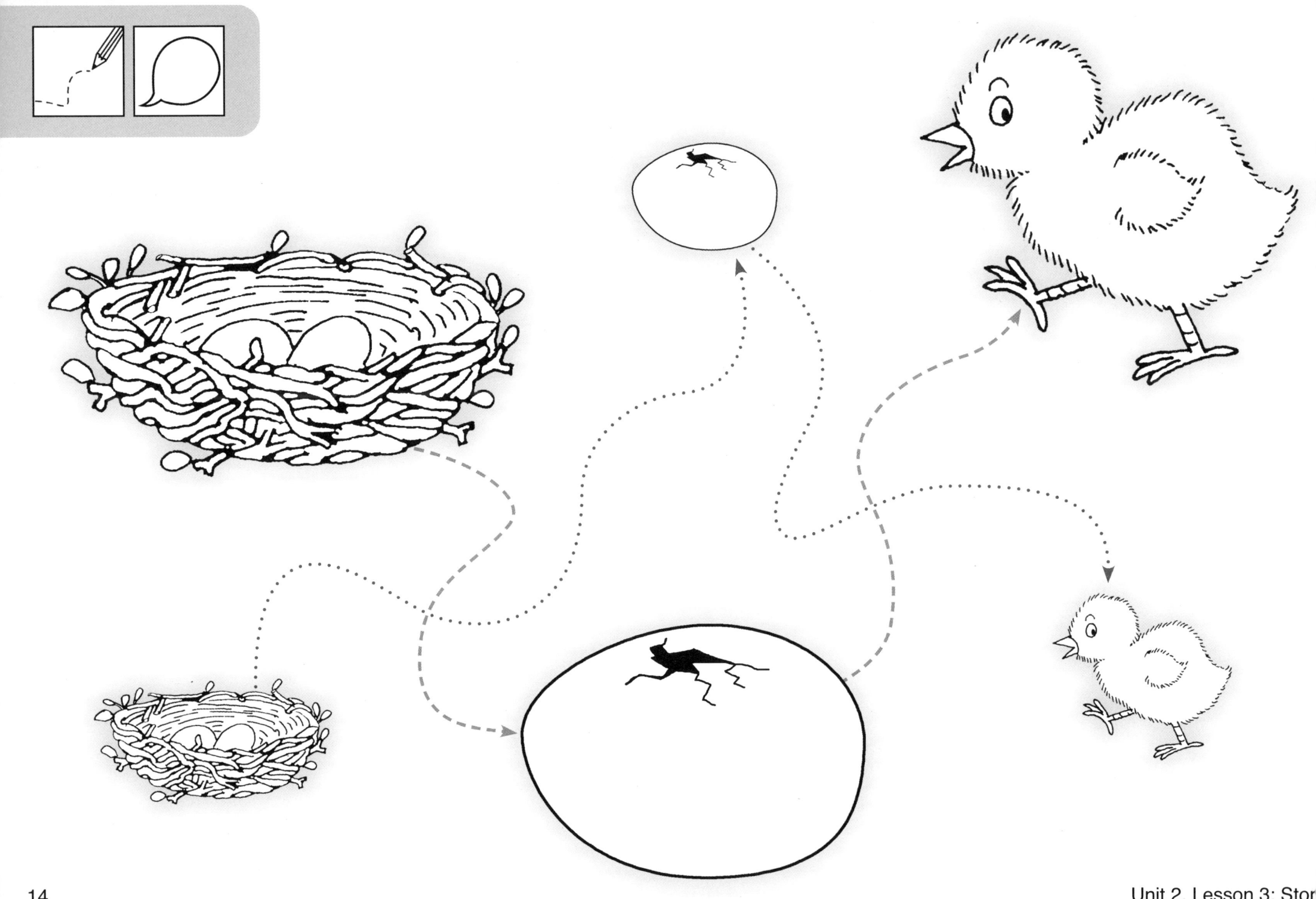

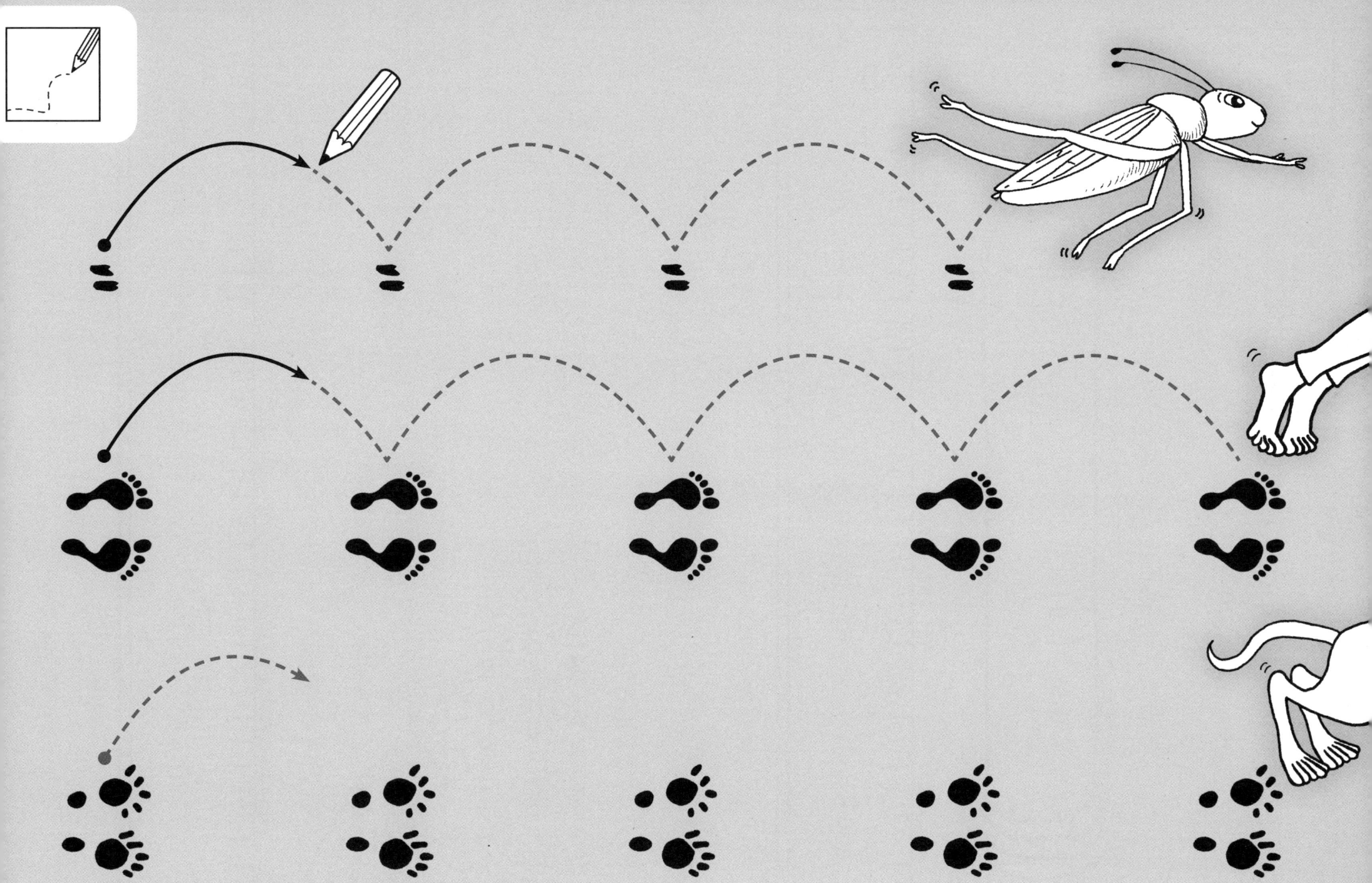

Unit 2, Lesson 4: Song

15

Review 2: /i/, /p/, /r

At the Farm

Unit 3, Lesson 1: Vocabulary

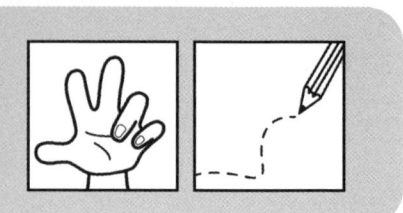

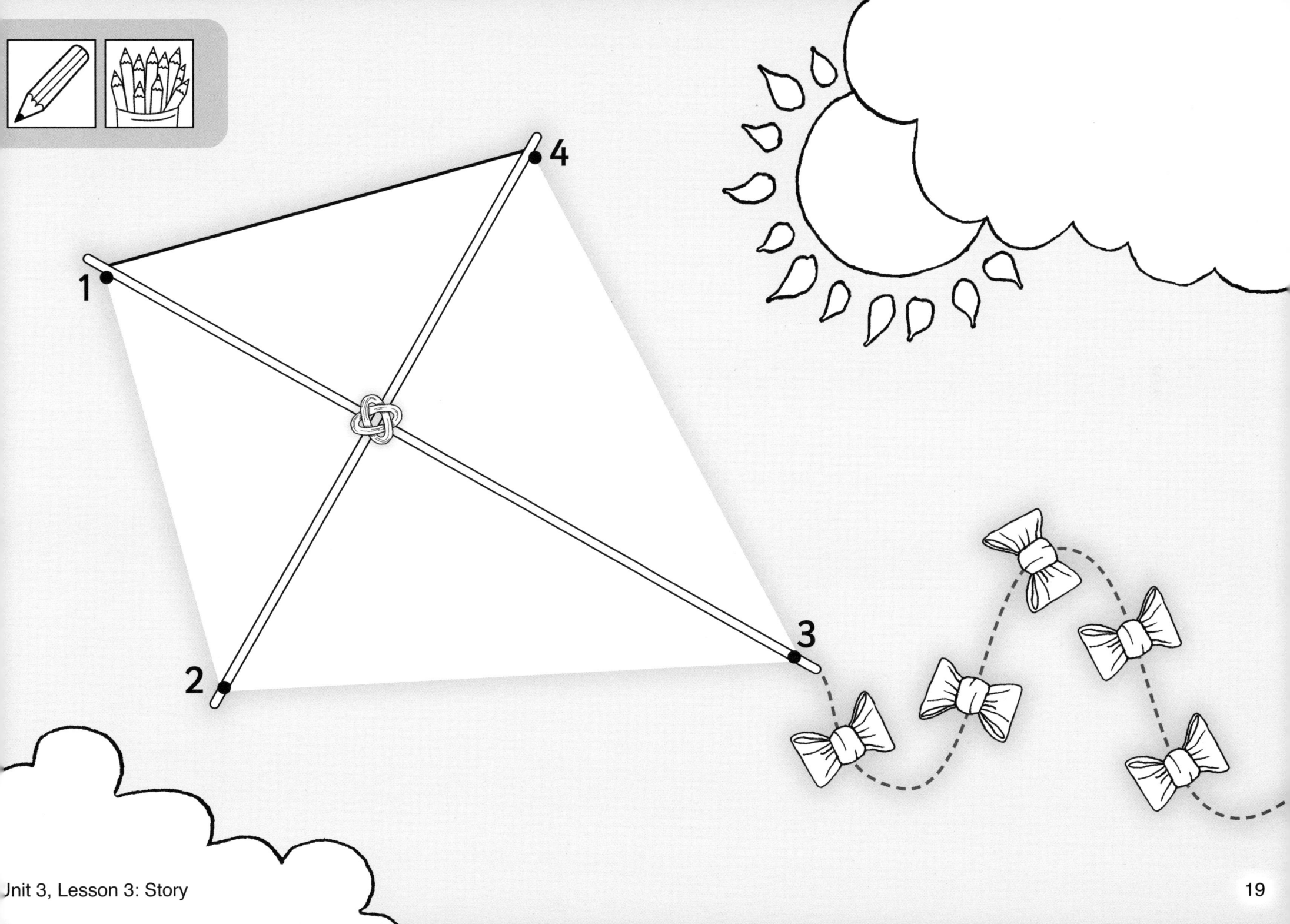

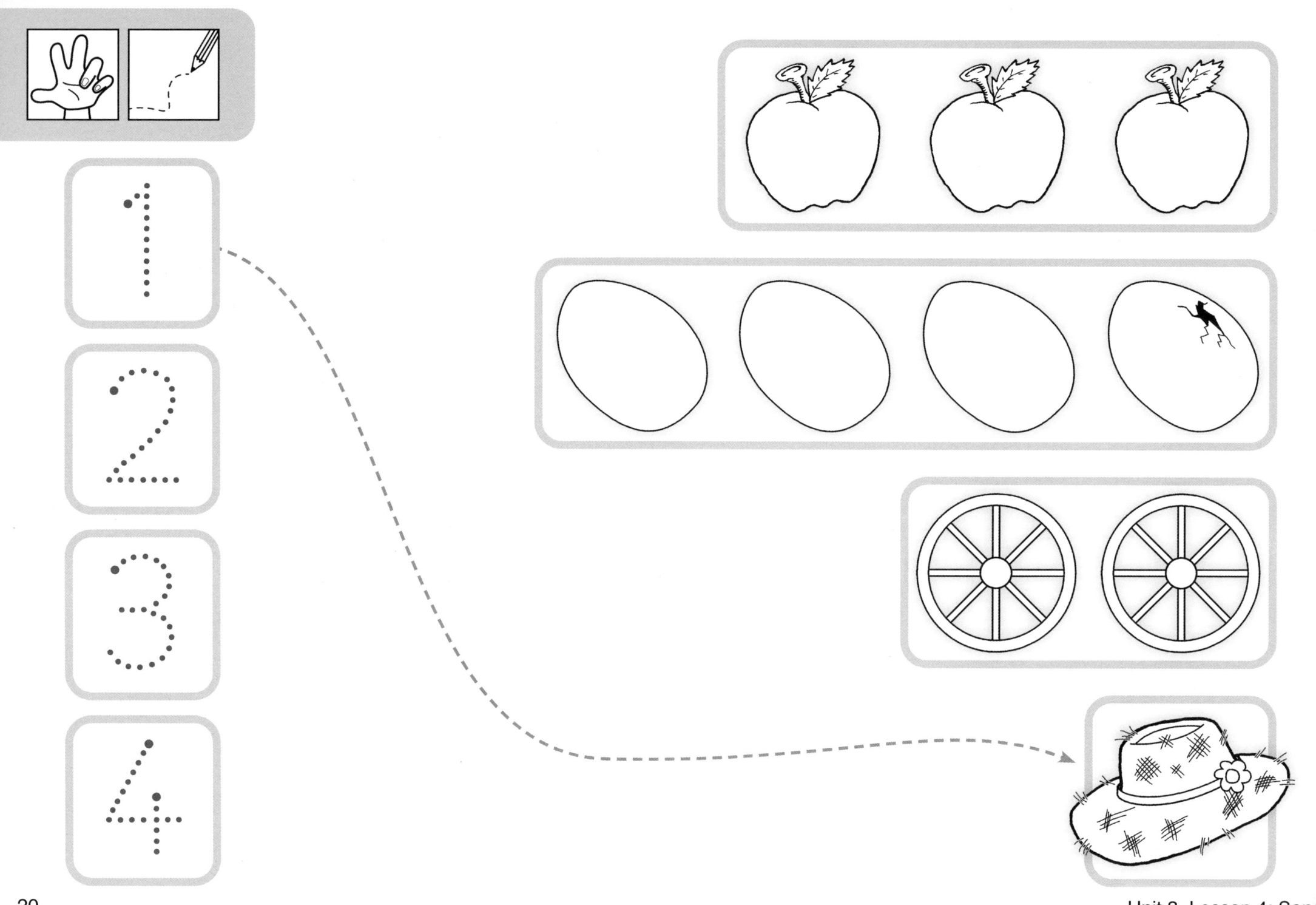

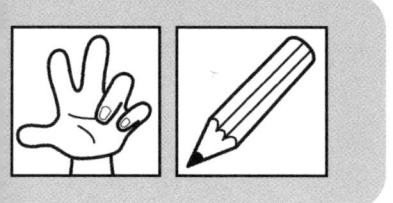    

Review 3: /c k/, /e/, /h/

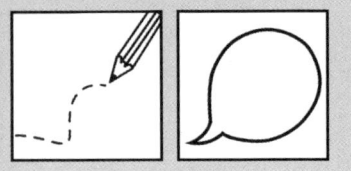

At Home

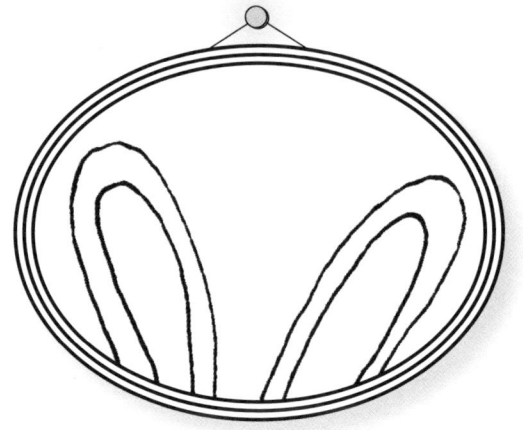

22   Unit 4, Lesson 1: Vocabulary

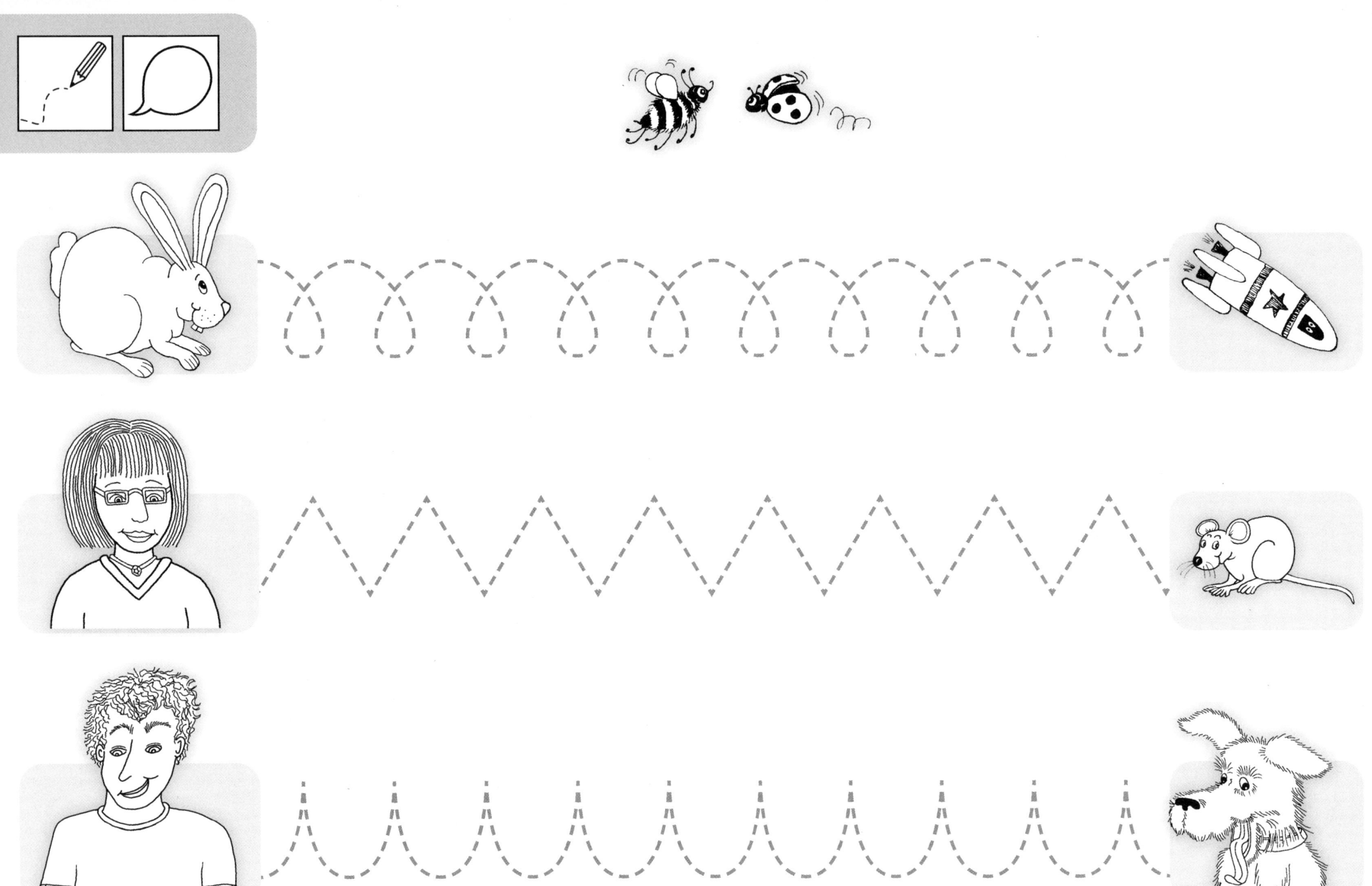

Review 4: /r/, /m/, /d/

 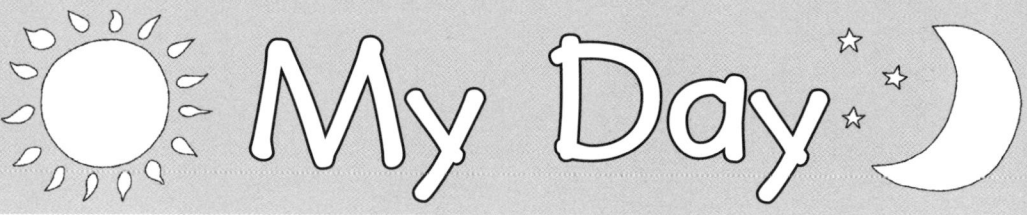

My Day

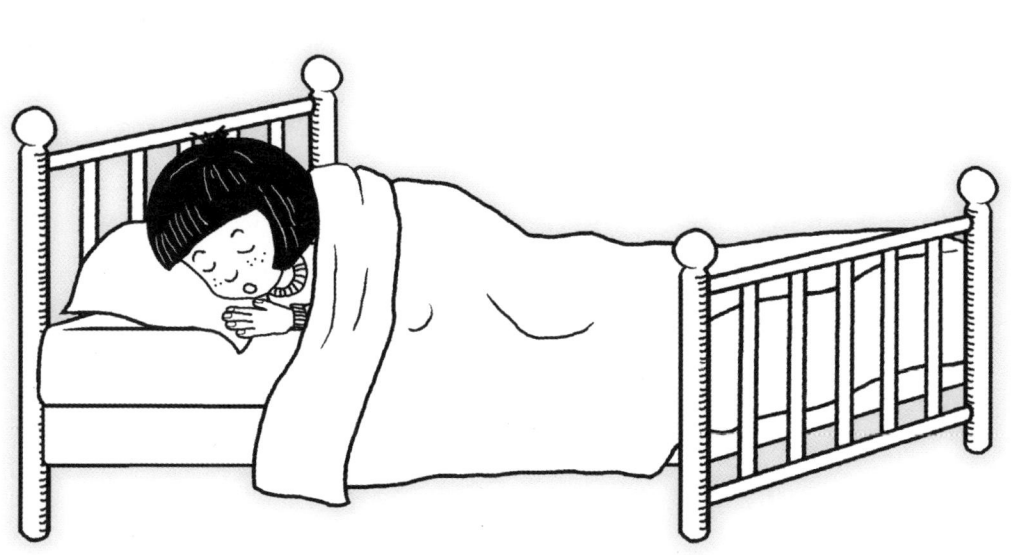 

Unit 5, Lesson 1: Vocabulary

Unit 5, Lesson 3: Story

Review 5: /g/, /o/, /u/, /l/

Unit 6, Lesson 2: Vocabulary

33

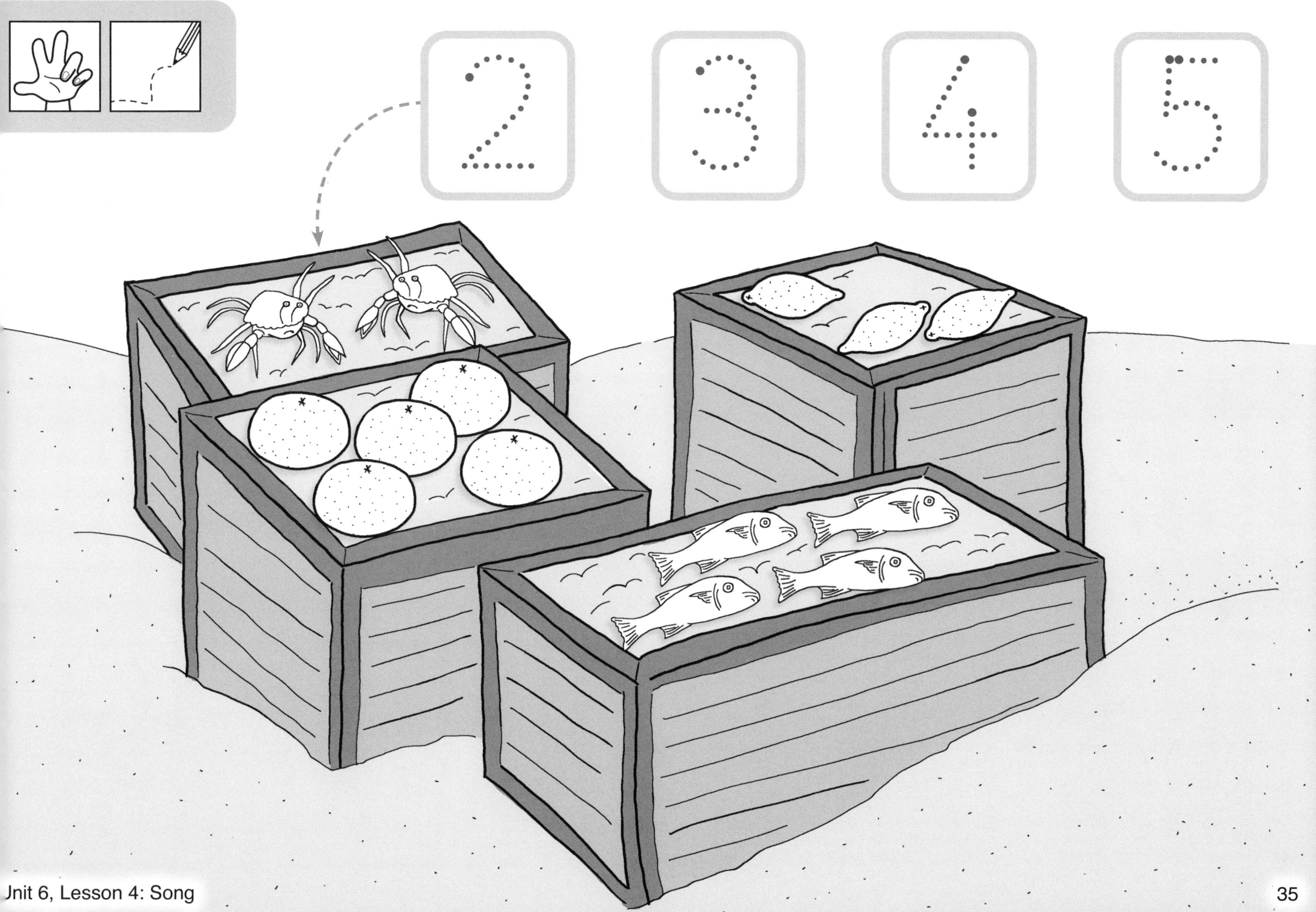

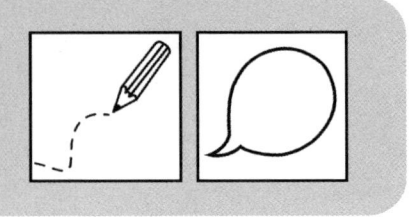

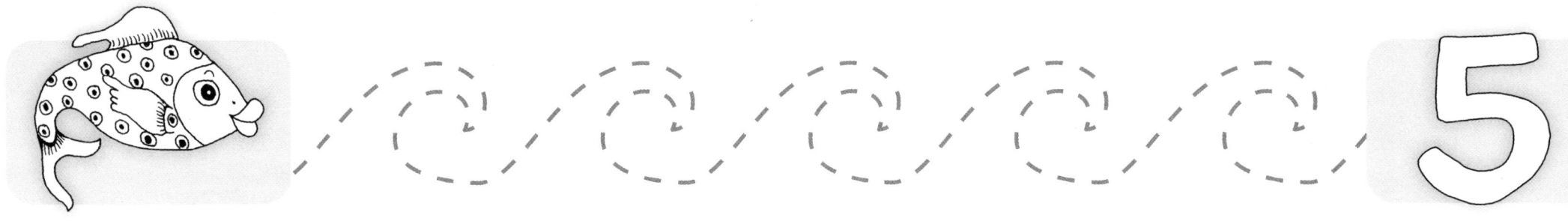
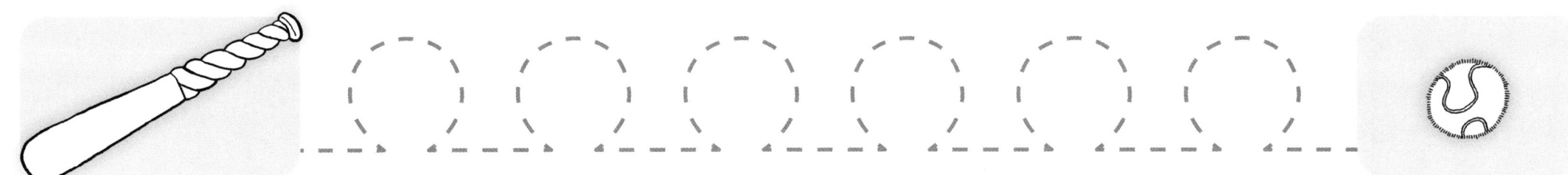

36   Review 6: /f/, /b/, /a

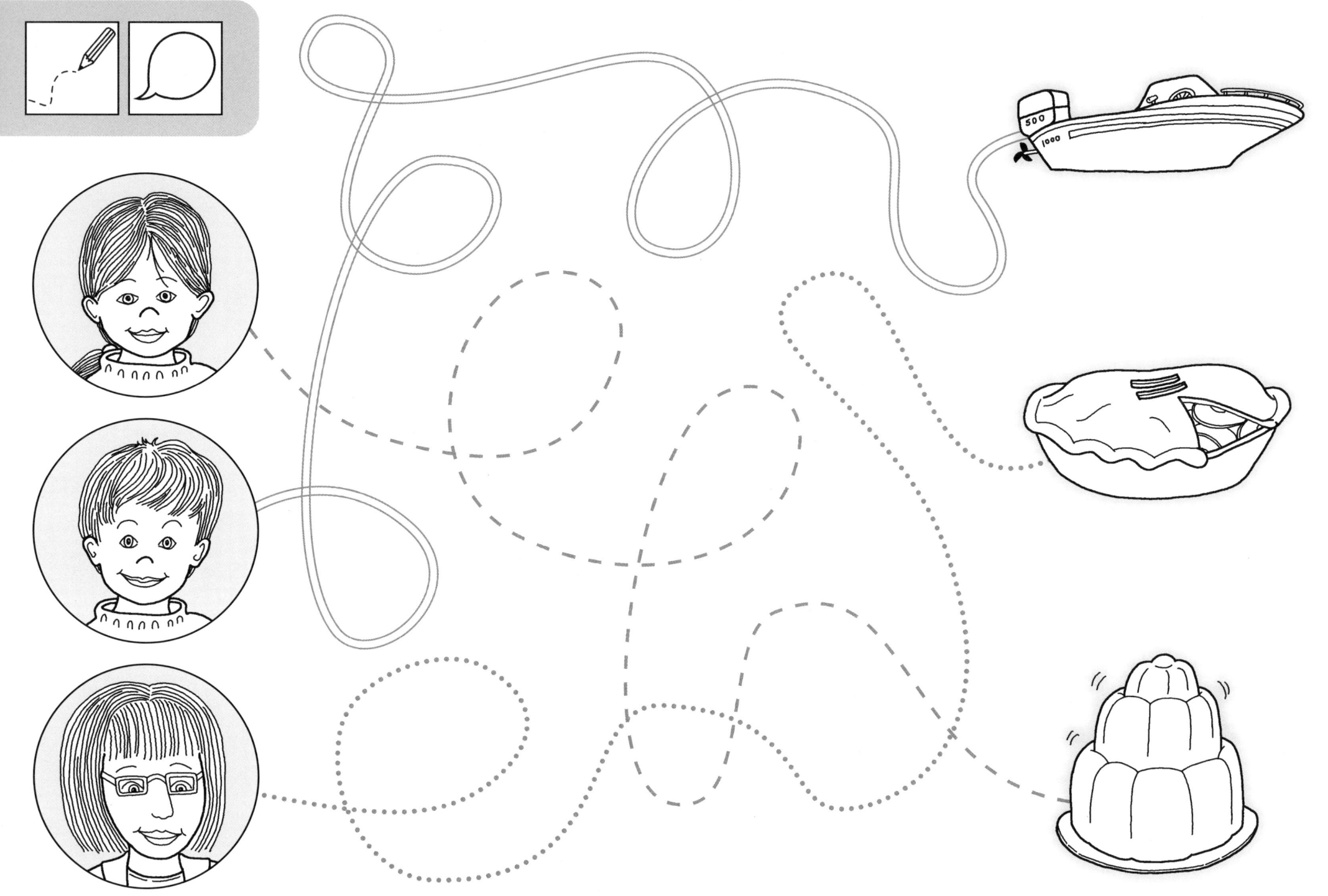

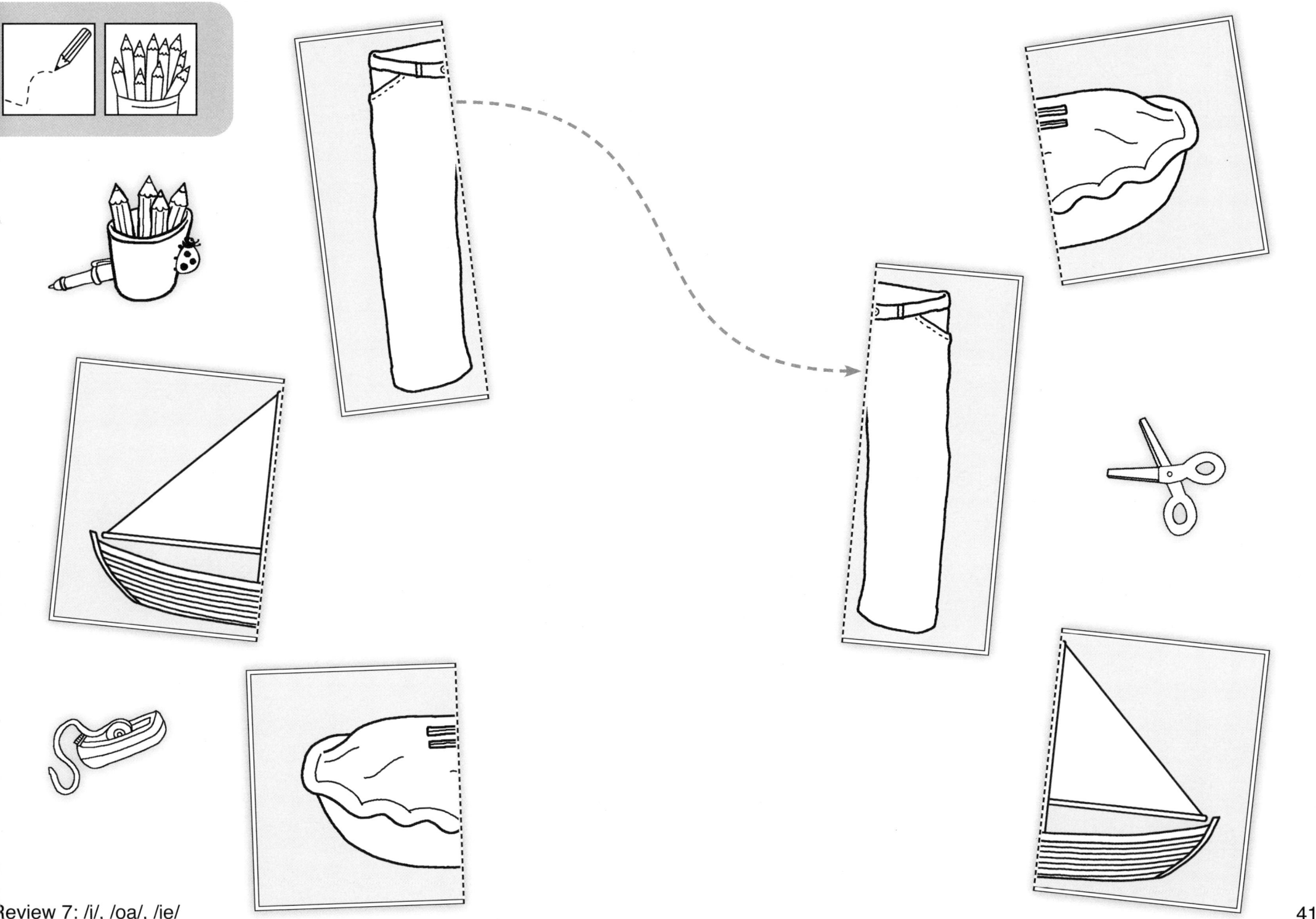

Review 7: /j/, /oa/, /ie/ 41

Animals

3

Unit 8, Lesson 1: Vocabulary

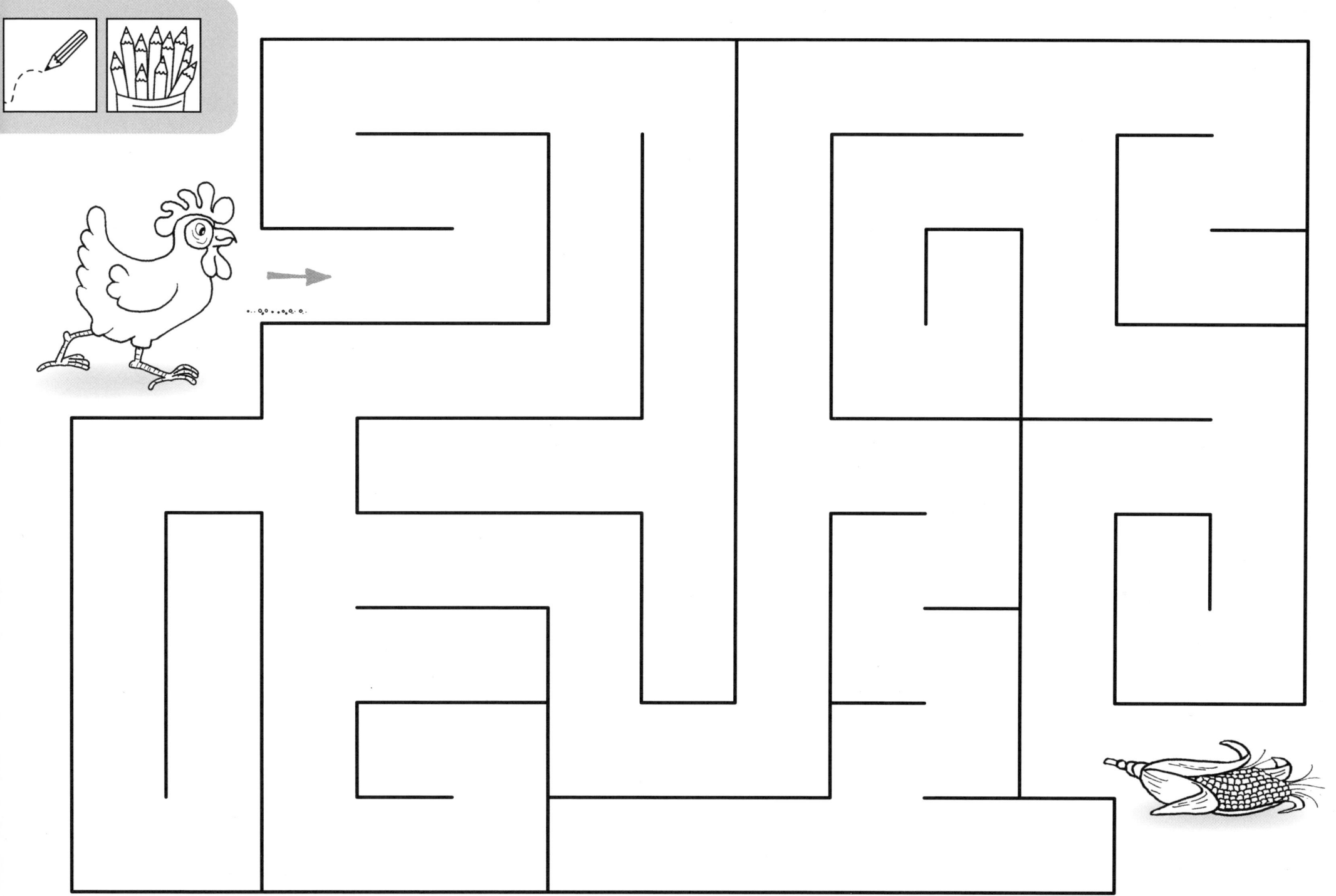

Unit 8, Lesson 2: Vocabulary

43

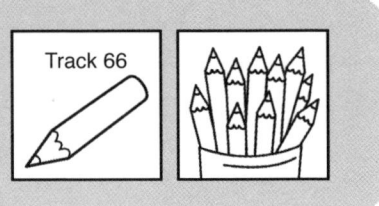

44 Unit 8, Lesson 3: Stor

Vocabulary Review

Toys

Food

Animals

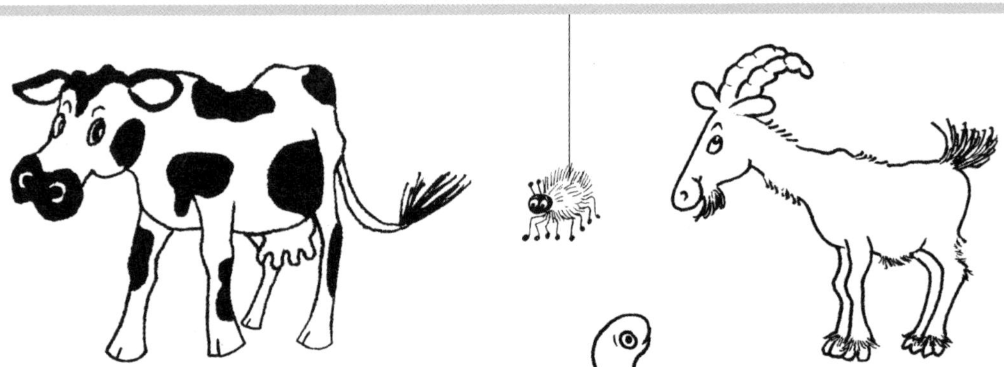

48 Vocabulary review